Your Initials	Date

Fran & Jesus

ON THE JOB

Mary Whelch

Tyndale House Publishers, Inc.
Wheaton, Illinois

Library of Congress Cataloging-in-Publication Data

Whelchel, Mary.
    Fran and Jesus on the job / Mary Whelchel.
       p.   cm.
    ISBN 0-8423-1226-9
    1. Single mothers—Religious life. 2. Widows—Religious life.
3. Women in business—Religious life. 4. Vocation. 5. Christian
life—1960- 6. Imaginary conversations. I. Title.
BV4596.S48W54   1993
248.8'431—dc20   93-9174

DEDICATION

To my best friend, Fran, whose life is very
different from the Fran in this book, but
whose childlike faith and willingness to be
open and vulnerable are indeed much like
this Fran. Through twenty-five years of
friendship you have been a wonderful and
encouraging role model of a simple, vibrant,
and real relationship with Jesus. Thanks,
Fran, for being my friend and my cheerleader.

TABLE OF CONTENTS

PREFACE   *vii*

CHAPTER **1**
   Facing the Fear of Job Hunting   *1*

CHAPTER **2**
   Fighting the Superwoman Syndrome   *22*

CHAPTER **3**
   Learning How to Witness   *41*

CHAPTER **4**
   Facing a Tough Ethical Decision   *65*

CHAPTER **5**
   Struggling with Singleness   *88*

CHAPTER **6**
   Recovering from Failure   *112*

CHAPTER **7**
   Battling Burnout and Stress   *125*

CHAPTER **8**
   Fretting over Finances   *143*

CHAPTER **9**
   Helping a Married Friend   *162*